Advanced English Conversation Dialogues:

Speak English Like a Native Speaker with Common Idioms and Phrases in American English

Jackie Bolen

Table of Contents

About the Author: Jackie Bolen

I taught English in South Korea for 10 years to every level and type of student. I've taught every age from kindergarten kids to adults. Most of my time has centered around teaching at two universities: five years at a science and engineering school in Cheonan, and four years at a major university in Busan where I taught upper level classes for students majoring in English. In my spare time, you can usually find me outside surfing, biking, hiking, or snowshoeing. I now live in Vancouver, Canada.

In case you were wondering what my academic qualifications are, I hold a Master of Arts in Psychology. During my time in Korea I successfully completed both the Cambridge CELTA and DELTA certification programs. With the combination of almost ten years teaching ESL/EFL learners of all ages and levels, and the more formal teaching qualifications I've obtained, I have a solid foundation on which to offer advice to English learners.

I truly hope that you find this book useful. I would love it if you sent me an email with any questions or feedback that you might have.

Jackie Bolen (www.jackiebolen.com)

Twitter: @bolen_jackie

Email: jb.business.online@gmail.com

This page intentionally left blank

Set #1: The Best of Both Worlds

Dialogue

Jerry: My friend Tommy **eats like a horse** but still doesn't gain any weight, **despite getting on in years**.

Linda: Lucky guy. I **eat like a bird** but still have to **watch my weight**. I do try to **spice things up** though with different kinds of salads and things like that.

Jerry: **Tough break!** I generally eat whatever I want but my wife can tell when I start to eat too much **junk food**!

Linda: Ideally, I'd have **the best of both worlds**. I could eat junk food but also not gain weight. It's not my **fate** though!

Vocabulary

The best of both worlds: Getting the benefits of two things at the same time. For example, having children but being able to afford a full-time nanny.

Spice things up: To make things more interesting or exciting.

Eat like a bird: To eat very little.

Eats like a horse: To eat a lot.

Getting on in years: Becoming older.

Tough break: When something unlucky or bad happens.

Junk food: Unhealthy food. For example, potato chips, fast food or candy.

Watch my weight: Gaining weight easily and having to be careful about what you eat.

Fate: Something that happens over which you have no control.

Exercise

Fill in the blanks with the correct phrase or idiom

1. She _____ but she's still so skinny.

2. I love to eat _____, especially while I'm watching TV.

3. I appreciate the fact that my teacher is trying to _____ a little bit but it comes across badly.

4. My doctor said that I have to _____.

5. Having grandchildren but not having to watch them all the time is _____.

6. I'm worried about my mom. She _____ these days.

7. The ball deflected in off the defence. What a _____.

8. My dad is _____ and may have to go to a care home.

9. My son thinks it's his _____ to take over the family business. But I do think he has a choice in this.

Answers:

1. eats like a horse

2. junk food

3. spice things up

4. watch my weight

5. the best of both worlds

6. eats like a bird

7. tough break

8. getting on in years

9. fate

Set #2: Speak of the Devil

Dialogue

Jerry: Have you seen Kenny lately? He **looks like a million bucks,** always wearing **flashy** clothes and driving his fancy new car.

Linda: I haven't seen him lately but guys like that are **a dime a dozen in this town.** They all made their money in finance, I think.

Jerry: **Speak of the devil!** I think I see him coming in the door right now! Let's call him over.

Linda: I don't want to **beat around the bush** so I'll just say it. I don't like Kenny! He **ripped me off** on his old TV that he sold me. It was hanging on by its' **last legs.**

Jerry: Let's **get out of here** then before he sees us.

Vocabulary

Speak of the devil: The person you are talking about appears at that exact moment. For example, you are talking about a coworker and then they walk into the room right then.

Looks like a million bucks: To look attractive or well put together.

A dime a dozen: Something that is very common, not special.

Beat around the bush: Avoid talking about something important, or not getting to the main point directly.

Ripped me off: To make a bad deal with someone. To be stolen from.

Get out of here: To leave a place, usually quickly.

Flashy: Bright, shiny, expensive.

Last legs: Something that is close to breaking/stopping/not working.

Exercise

Fill in the blanks with the correct phrase or idiom

1. Tim _____ these days with his new haircut.

2. Job offers like that are _____.

3. I want to _____ so badly! I hate this school.

4. "Oh, _____! We were just talking about you!"

5. Honestly, I hate that my boss loves to _____. I wish he'd just get to the point.

6. I'm so embarrassed that he_____.

7. My brother got a _____ new haircut in preparation for his job interview.

8. I'm going to have to buy a new car. This one is on its' _____.

Answers:

1. looks like a million bucks

2. a dime a dozen

3. get out of here

4. speak of the devil

5. beat around the bush

6. ripped me off

7. flashy

8. last legs

Set #3: See Eye to Eye

Dialogue

Jerry: I don't want to **make waves** here, but I don't think your friend is making a good financial decision.

Linda: Oh, I don't know. Maybe you just don't see **eye to eye**? I think she's done a lot of research and **knows what she's doing**.

Jerry: Well, I understand why you'd think that. You were **born with a silver spoon in your mouth**, just like your friend. Anyway, it's some **food for thought**! I'm personally hoping to avoid making the same mistake as your friend.

Linda: To play the **Devil's advocate**, you might do well to reconsider your own financial decisions.

Jerry: Hmmm...okay. Let's **agree to disagree**. We're never going to **settle** this over a beer.

Vocabulary

See eye to eye: Agreeing with someone.

Born with a silver spoon in your mouth: Someone who comes from a wealthy family who doesn't have to work that hard in life.

Food for thought: Something to think about.

Make waves: To cause trouble.

Devil's advocate: Taking the other side in an argument.

Knows what she's doing: To be sure of something or do something correctly.

Agree to disagree: To stop talking about something controversial when you can't come to an agreement.

Settle: Decide or agree to something.

Exercise

Fill in the blanks with the correct phrase or idiom

1. My mom and I had to finally _____ because there was no way we could understand each other's point of view.

2. I'm not trying to _____ but I just don't agree with what's going on at my company.

3. I'm thinking about changing jobs. My boss and I don't _____.

4. My cousin was _____ and has never had to work a day in his life.

5. My younger brother's most annoying habit is his need to always play the _____.

6. That newspaper article had some _____ in it.

7. My teacher _____. I've learned so much from her.

8. I was hoping to not have to _____ for that job because the salary isn't great but it's tough in this economy.

Answers:

1. agree to disagree

2. make waves

3. see eye to eye

4. born with a silver spoon in his mouth

5. Devil's advocate

6. food for thought

7. knows what she's doing

8. settle

Set #4: Once in a Blue Moon

Dialogue

Jerry: Why are all of our coworkers **living hand to mouth**? We get paid a **living wage. I can't make heads nor tails of it**.

Linda: Well, I think most of them **hit the bottle** pretty hard after work every day. That **costs a pretty penny**. But, your **guess is as good as mine**.

Jerry: I've noticed that too. I used to **drink a lot** but now it's only **once in a blue moon**. I had to **quit cold turkey** for a couple of years before I could **get a handle on it**.

Linda: Good for you for making a big change like that! Plus, it's saved you a lot of money I'm sure.

Vocabulary

Once in a blue moon: Something that doesn't happen often.

Quit cold turkey: Suddenly stop doing something addictive. Most commonly refers to smoking.

Living hand to mouth: To live paycheck to paycheck. Not having lots of money, especially disposable income.

Living wage: Salary that is high enough to cover all the monthly bills relatively easily.

Your guess is as good as mine: To not know something.

Hit the bottle: Drink alcohol.

Get a handle on it: To control something.

Costs a pretty penny: Is expensive.

Can't make heads nor tails of it: Unable to understand something.

Drink a lot: Consume lots of alcohol.

12

Exercise

Fill in the blanks with the correct phrase or idiom

1. My dad _____ hard when I was a kid.

2. That new car I want _____.

3. I'm going back to school so can find a job that pays a _____.

4. I only eat junk food _____.

5. I want to quit smoking but it's difficult to _____.

6. I've heard that the best way to stop smoking is to _____.

7. It's often hard for single parents to avoid _____.

8. Math just isn't my subject! I _____.

9. Wow! They sure do _____.

Answers:

1. hit the bottle

2. costs a pretty penny

3. living wage

4. once in a blue moon

5. get a handle on it

6. quit cold turkey

7. living hand to mouth

8. can't make heads nor tails of it

9. drink a lot

Set #5: When Pigs Fly

Dialogue

Jerry: My kids are **buttering me up** because they don't want to have to help put up **Christmas lights.**

Linda: You're lucky that you can get some help **once in a while**. My kids never **pitch in** for stuff like that. **When pigs fly**, right?

Jerry: Ah, it's all **smoke and mirrors** at my house usually. My kids **make a show out of** cleaning up after themselves after dinner but their rooms are still like a **pigsty**.

Linda: What have we gotten ourselves into?

Vocabulary

When pigs fly: Something that is very unlikely to happen.

Pitch in: To contribute to or help with something.

Buttering me up: To flatter or please someone because you want something in return. For example, a child who is extra nice to their parents around Christmas because they want an expensive video game system.

Smoke and mirrors: Flashy things that distract from what is real.

Christmas lights: Lights on houses for decoration around Christmas.

Once in a while: Sometimes.

Make a show out of: To do something in a flashy way.

Pigsty: Usually refers to a very messy room or space.

Exercise

Fill in the blanks with the correct phrase or idiom

1. I like to let loose _____.

2. His presentation was all _____. No real substance.

3. My kids love to help me put up _____.

4. We all _____ every Saturday morning to clean up the house.

5. My kid's bedroom is a _____.

6. My mom always used to say, "_____" when I asked her for money!

7. I know when my kids are _____ but I fall for it anyway. Their sweet smiles!

8. I hate that my coworkers always _____ finishing even the smallest task.

Answers:

1. once in a while

2. smoke and mirrors

3. Christmas lights

4. pitch in

5. pigsty

6. When pigs fly

7. buttering me up

8. make a show out of

Set #6: Cost an arm and a leg

Dialogue

Jerry: Hey Linda, don't **jump the gun** on buying a car. They **cost an arm and a leg**. It's wise to do some research first. A good **rule of thumb** is one hour of research for every $500 you plan to spend on something!

Linda: You're such a **smart cookie**. I'm glad to call you a friend. What would I do without you?

Jerry: I'm not sure! But, you're a really good **shoulder to cry on** and you've been with me through **thick and thin**. I appreciate you too!

Linda: Well, **birds of a feather flock together**. We have so much in common it's impossible not to be friends!

Vocabulary

Cost an arm and a leg: Very expensive.

Rule of thumb: A general, unwritten rule about something.

Smart cookie: An intelligent person.

Jump the gun: Do something too quickly.

Shoulder to cry on: Someone that offers comfort in a difficult situation.

Thick and thin: Through good and bad times.

Birds of a feather flock together: Good friends who are there for each other.

Exercise

Fill in the blanks with the correct phrase or idiom

1. My brother is a _____. He always got top marks in school.

2. My husband and I have been together through _____.

3. New cars these days _____.

4. He's always ready to _____ but it'd do him well to be a bit more patient.

5. My _____ is to always turn off the lights when I leave a room.

6. Today, I need a _____.

7. My dad always used to say, "_____" to talk about my brother and I. We'd never tattle on each other no matter what.

Answers:

1. smart cookie

2. thick and thin

3. cost an arm and a leg

4. jump the gun

5. rule of thumb

6. shoulder to cry on

7. birds of a feather flock together

Set #7: A Piece of Cake

Dialogue

Jerry: I'm thinking about running a marathon. I have **butterflies in my stomach** though. It's going to be difficult!

Linda: What? It'll be **a piece of cake** for you. You're **as fit as a fiddle**.

Jerry: I know I'm always **cool as a cucumber** when I start the race but then I get so tired in the middle. I eventually get a **second wind** though.

Linda: **Fingers crossed** that you'll **knock 'em dead**. I'll come to cheer for you!

Jerry: What about you? Did the doctor give you **a clean bill of health**? You can train with me.

Linda: I'm not quite **back on my feet** yet. Maybe in a few weeks, we can talk about running together.

Vocabulary

A piece of cake: Something that's easy to do.

Cool as a cucumber: Someone who is very calm or relaxed.

As fit as a fiddle: In really good shape.

Second wind: Having some energy again after being tired. Usually applies to exercise or staying up late.

Butterflies in my stomach: To feel nervous about something.

Fingers crossed: To wish someone good luck. Or, a symbol of good luck.

Knock 'em dead: Do well or be successful at an event.

A clean bill of health: Healthy, not sick anymore.

Back on my feet: Recovered, after a problem (health, financial, divorce, etc.)

Exercise

Fill in the blanks with the correct phrase or idiom

1. Don't worry, I'm sure you'll _____.

2. Under pressure, Roger Federer is as _____.

3. I always get _____ before a test.

4. That speaking test was _____.

5. I've got my _____ waiting for the results of the SAT.

6. My grandpa is _____ even though he is 80.

7. I hope I get my _____. I have lots more studying to do!

8. I'm hoping to get _____ after my recent job loss.

9. I'm hoping that the doctors give me _____.

Answers:

1. knock 'em dead

2. cool as a cucumber

3. butterflies in my stomach

4. a piece of cake

5. fingers crossed

6. as fit as a fiddle

7. second wind

8. back on my feet

9. a clean bill of health

Set #8: Let the Cat Out of the Bag

Dialogue

Jerry: I want to **nip this in the bud** now that the **cat is out of the bag**. I don't want people talking about me at work.

Linda: Oh, **spill the beans** Jerry. I haven't heard anything about it.

Jerry: Well, I'm thinking about leaving the company but nothing is final yet. I do have some **irons in the fire** though. I don't want people talking about it because I may end up staying here.

Linda: **Say no more. Your secret is safe with me**.

Jerry: Thanks Linda, we're definitely **on the same wavelength**.

Vocabulary

The cat is out of the bag: Accidentally reveal something secret.

Spill the beans: To tell a secret.

Nip this in the bud: To stop something bad from happening early on in the process.

Irons in the fire: A few different plans.

Say no more: The matter is finished or decided.

Your secret is safe with me: Not telling a secret to other people.

On the same wavelength: To have similar thinking about something.

Exercise

Fill in the blanks with the correct phrase or idiom

1. _____. I'm on top of this right now.

2. I can tell you now that _____.

3. I want to _____ before it becomes a much bigger issue.

4. Come on! Just _____, please!

5. My dad has so many _____ with all his side-gigs.

6. Don't worry about it! _____.

7. My husband and I just aren't _____ about having kids.

Answers:

1. say no more

2. the cat is out of the bag

3. nip this in the bud

4. spill the beans

5. irons in the fire

6. your secret is safe with me

7. on the same wavelength

Set #9: Feeling Under the Weather

Dialogue

Jerry: I know, I know. My mom used to tell me to not be such a **couch potato** and that **an apple a day keeps the doctor away**. I wish that I'd listened to her! I'm feeling **worse for wear.**

Linda: **Keep your chin up**! I know you're **feeling under the weather** but **this too shall pass.**

Jerry: Thanks Linda, I appreciate you **checking in on** me every day.

Linda: **It's the least I can do**. You've helped me with so many things over the years. Just don't **kick the bucket** on me, okay?

Vocabulary

Feeling under the weather: Not feeling well; feeling sick.

Keep your chin up: Telling something to stay strong. Encouraging someone in a tough situation.

Couch potato: Someone who spends lots of time on the couch watching TV or movies or playing video games. Not active.

An apple a day keeps the doctor away: Eating healthy keeps you from getting sick.

This too shall pass: A bad period of time that will eventually end.

Checking in on: To see how someone is doing.

It's the least I can do: No problem; it's a small thing, usually when you feel like you should do more.

Worse for wear: Feeling worn out or tired.

Kick the bucket: Die.

Exercise

Fill in the blanks with the correct phrase or idiom

1. My dad keeps phoning and _____ me. It's almost too much!

2. I keep nagging my son to get active because he's such a _____.

3. I called in sick because I was feeling a bit _____.

4. My mom is great at telling people to _____ when something bad happens.

5. I'm convinced that the saying, "_____" really does work!

6. My son has been pretty down lately but I told him that, "_____."

7. Lunch is on me. _____, seeing as you've been making me meals all week.

8. I'm _____ after being in the hospital for more than a week. It was impossible to sleep there.

9. I hope that I don't _____ before I'm 80 but I'm nervous about how much I smoke!

Answers:

1. checking in on

2. couch potato

3. under the weather

4. keep your chin up

5. An apple a day keeps the doctor away

6. This too shall pass

7. It's the least I can do

8. worse for wear

9. kick the bucket

Set #10: Kill Two Birds with One Stone

Dialogue

Jerry: I think I've found a way that I can **kill two birds with one stone** on this project at work. It's a little bit **sketchy** though.

Linda: Oh Jerry, you know that stuff like that **isn't my cup of tea**. I like to keep everything **aboveboard**.

Jerry: Yeah, I know. You're always on the **up and up**. But I don't mind **crossing the line** once in a while.

Linda: Well, keep me **out of the loop**! I don't want to hear any more about it.

Jerry: Okay, okay! I know you do everything **by the book**. I'll talk to Kenny about it. He likes to **think outside the box** about this kind of stuff.

Vocabulary

Kill two birds with one stone: Solving two problems at the same time. For example, using the same essay for two different university classes.

Isn't my cup of tea: Something that you wouldn't do. For example, you have a friend who loves skydiving but you have no interest in it.

Up and up: Not illegal or sketchy.

Aboveboard: Not illegal or sketchy.

Crossing the line: Illegal or not quite honest/right.

Out of the loop: Not knowing anything about it.

Sketchy: Not completely legal or right.

By the book: Completely legal, doing something the correct way.

Think outside the box: Someone who has a different way of thinking about something than most people.

Exercise

Fill in the blanks with the correct phrase or idiom

1. He's been _____ a lot lately. I'm not surprised that he finally got caught.

2. That popular new TV show just _____.

3. I remember him being pretty sketchy but he seems like he's on the _____ now.

4. Am I the only one who didn't know she was pregnant? I'm so _____.

5. I wish my company was a bit more _____. It's a bit difficult to work for them sometimes.

6. I'm hoping to _____ to potentially save myself a lot of time.

7. My Internet provider seems a little bit _____ but I love how cheap they are.

8. One of the things that frustrate me about my wife is that she does everything completely _____.

9. Let's try to _____ about this problem.

Answers:

1. crossing the line

2. isn't my cup of tea

3. up and up

4. out of the loop

5. aboveboard

6. kill two birds with one stone

7. sketchy

8. by the book

9. think outside the box

Set #11: Cutting Corners

Dialogue

Jerry: My company has been **cutting corners** on this latest project and we're **in hot water** now.

Linda: Well, honestly, it's time for your company to **face the music.** You've been doing some things that cross the line for years now.

Jerry: Hey, hey. I know. You're **barking up the wrong tree**! I don't have anything to do with making the decisions. I do what I'm told. I'm basically a **yes man.**

Linda: I know. But, I wish you'd find some **greener pastures**. That company is going to **go under** soon I think.

Jerry: Well, jobs in my field are like a **needle in a haystack** these days. I'd leave if I could.

Vocabulary

Cutting Corners: Doing something cheaply or badly. Can often be related to construction/home renovations.

Face the music: Deal with the reality of something negative that you did. For example, getting punished for a crime.

In hot water: In trouble for something.

Barking up the wrong tree: Blaming someone for something that isn't their fault.

Greener pastures: A better opportunity.

Go under: Go bankrupt or out of business.

Yes man: A weak person who always agrees with their superior at work or in politics.

Needle in a haystack: Something that is impossible to find.

Exercise

Fill in the blanks with the correct phrase or idiom

1. That CEO made some terrible decisions and his company is about to _____.

2. I'm leaving my job and heading for _____.

3. It's time to _____ for ripping all those customers off.

4. Honestly, you're _____. Johnny did it, not me.

5. Donald Trump is _____ these days with the most recent scandal.

6. The guy painting my house is _____. I feel so angry about it.

7. I hate that my husband is forced into being a _____ in his new role at the company.

8. Looking for my glasses in my messy house is like finding a _____.

Answers:

1. go under

2. greener pastures

3. face the music

4. barking up the wrong tree

5. in hot water

6. cutting corners

7. yes man

8. needle in a haystack

Set #12: Add Insult to Injury

Dialogue

Jerry: To **add insult to injury**, my dad got Covid-19 when he was in the hospital for a heart attack.

Linda: Oh no. Is he okay?

Jerry: Well, he's not **out of the woods** yet. He's still **sick as a dog** but he's not **at death's door**.

Linda: Okay, good to hear. Send him my **best wishes**, okay?

Jerry: **Don't waste your breath**. He still acts like he got up on the **wrong side of the bed** all the time.

Linda: Well, you certainly don't **take after** him. Don't worry!

Vocabulary

Add insult to Injury: Make something already bad worse. For example, a guy fell off his bike but then a car ran over his foot.

Out of the woods: A difficult situation that has improved. Usually refers to medical things when someone is very sick but has recovered a little bit.

Don't waste your breath: Whatever you say doesn't make a difference.

Sick as a dog: Very unwell.

At death's door: Close to dying.

Wrong side of the bed: Grumpy.

Best wishes: Friendly hope that someone is doing well.

Take after: Usually a son/daughter who is similar to his/her mother/father.

Exercise

Fill in the blanks with the correct phrase or idiom

1. My sister hates mornings and often gets up on the _____.

2. I was _____ last year and spent a week in the hospital.

3. He's doing better but he's not _____ yet.

4. I can't believe he made it! He was _____.

5. _____. I've already made up my mind.

6. I honestly don't want to _____ but it looks like you have a flat tire too.

7. _____ on your recent engagement!

8. I hope my son doesn't _____ me. I haven't been the best example for him growing up.

Answers:

1. wrong side of the bed

2. sick as a dog

3. out of the woods

4. at death's door

5. Don't waste your breath

6. add insult to injury

7. Best wishes

8. take after

Set #13: You can't Judge a Book by Its Cover

Dialogue

Jerry: Have you met our new neighbor yet?

Linda: I talked to him last night but he's **a hard nut to crack**. He only gave one-word answers to all my questions!

Jerry: Well, **you can't judge a book by its cover**. I'm sure we'll find out more about him as time goes on. Maybe he's not that **talkative.**

Linda: Maybe. But I felt frustrated talking to him for just a few minutes. Anyway, I'm working on not **burning bridges** so I'll **put my best foot forward**!

Jerry: Good plan. You never know **what may come**. Let's invite him over for dinner and see if he **opens up**.

Vocabulary

You can't judge a book by its cover: to not judge something or someone based on appearance. For example, a restaurant that's not stylish and new may have delicious food.

A hard nut to crack: Someone that is difficult to get to know.

Burning bridges: Damaging relationships.

Put my best foot forward: To be on one's best behaviour.

What may come: What could happen in the future.

Talkative: Someone who likes to talk a lot.

Opens up: Shares information about oneself.

Exercise

Fill in the blanks with the correct phrase or idiom

1. I try my best to avoid _____ when leaving a job.

2. I'm happy for the fresh start and want to _____ at this new job.

3. My dad rarely talks and is _____.

4. I learned early on in life that _____.

5. I'm well prepared for _____.

6. My daughter is so _____. I go for a walk every day to get a break!

7. I love it when my son _____ to me. It happens so rarely!

Answers:

1. burning bridges

2. put my best foot forward

3. a hard nut to crack

4. you can't judge a book by its cover

5. what may come

6. talkative

7. opens up

Set #14: Break a Leg

Dialogue

Jerry: Hey, I heard **through the grapevine** that you're going to be in a play next month.

Linda: It's true. I must admit! I had to **blow off some steam** from work and escaping into my character is a great way to do that.

Jerry: You're really **taking the bull by the horns** lately! Can I come watch?

Linda: Sure, **knock yourself out**! It's a little bit **amateur hour** but **on the upside**, the tickets are cheap!

Jerry: Okay, I'll come for sure. I can't forget to tell you to **break a leg** though!

Vocabulary

Break a leg: To wish someone good luck, usually before performing or going on stage.

Blow off some steam: Doing something to get rid of stress. For example, having a few drinks after a difficult work project.

Knock yourself out: To try hard to do something. Often something that others think is a waste of time.

Taking the bull by the horns: Doing something bravely and decisively.

Through the grapevine: To spread information informally. Often related to gossip.

Amateur hour: Not professional.

On the upside: Something positive in a generally negative situation.

Exercise

Fill in the blanks with the correct phrase or idiom

1. I heard _____ that Tom and Monica broke up.

2. You want to do that for me? _____.

3. I starting playing soccer to _____ from my terrible job.

4. Well, _____, this job has better hours.

5. Good luck and _____.

6. It was hard to watch that presentation. Talk about _____.

7. I'm _____ at work lately and it's going well!

Answers:

1. through the grapevine

2. Knock yourself out

3. blow off some steam

4. on the upside

5. break a leg

6. amateur hour

7. taking the bull by the horns

Set #15: Hit the Nail on the Head

Dialogue

Jerry: Let's **cut to the chase** here. Ben is going **off his rocker** and I don't even understand half the stuff he's saying.

Linda: **What's his deal** do you think?

Jerry: Maybe dementia? He's **getting on in years**.

Linda: Hmmm...you may have **hit the nail on the head**. Maybe we should **get in touch with** his daughter? I'm not sure she knows what happening.

Jerry: Good idea. I'll **give her a ring** this week.

Vocabulary

Hit the nail on the head: To describe exactly what is causing a situation or problem. For example, a technician hit the nail on the head when she discovered that all the tech problems were caused by a poor Internet connection.

Cut to the chase: Getting to the important things instead of all the minor details. For example, someone who is nervous about talking about a problem with their husband or wife might "beat around the bush" instead of cutting to the chase.

Off his rocker: Someone who is acting crazy or not rationally.

What's his deal?: What's wrong with him?

Getting on in years: Becoming older.

Get in touch with: Contact someone.

Give her a ring: Call someone by phone.

Exercise

Fill in the blanks with the correct phrase or idiom

1. He's been acting very strangely lately. _____?

2. Tommy, I think you've _____. Everything is clearer now.

3. Let's _____ and stop beating around the bush.

4. My grandfather is _____.

5. It took him a long time to _____ me.

6. I think the president of that company is kind of _____.

7. Don't forget to _____. You need to talk about the Christmas party.

Answers:

1. What's his deal

2. hit the nail on the head

3. cut to the chase

4. getting on in years

5. get in touch with

6. off his rocker

7. give her a ring

Set #16: Blessing in Disguise

Dialogue

Jerry: Did you hear that Beth **got canned** last month?

Linda: Oh wow! **No kidding**.

Jerry: It turned out to be a **blessing in disguise** though. She got a higher-paying job **lickety-split.**

Linda: Oh, that's great. She wasn't **living within her means**, **splashing out** all the time. Maybe this will solve her **financial woes**.

Jerry: **Time will tell!** I'll have to **see it to believe it.**

Linda: Well, at least she gets to start with a **clean slate**. It's a good opportunity for her.

Vocabulary

Blessing in Disguise: Something that initially seems bad which turns out good in the end. For example, someone lost their job but ended up getting a better job three months later.

Live within her means: To not spend more than she makes.

Got canned: Fired from a job.

No kidding: A response to something surprising.

In no time: Quickly.

Splashing out: Spending extravagantly.

Financial woes: Money trouble.

Lickety-split: Quickly.

Time will tell: Wait and see.

See it to believe it: When you don't think something is likely.

Clean slate: New beginning.

Exercise

Fill in the blanks with the correct phrase or idiom

1. Be patient. _____ if that was a good decision or not.

2. Do you honestly think that he's changed? I'll have to _____.

3. Wow, _____. I can't believe I won the contest!

4. My brother _____ because he was always late for work.

5. Are you sure you want to buy dinner? You're really _____.

6. Maybe getting fired was a _____. I hated that job.

7. I'm trying to teach my wife to _____ but it's an uphill battle.

8. I'm embarrassed to admit it, but all of our _____ were caused by me.

9. I'll get to it _____. Don't worry.

10. I had the project done _____ but my boss still wasn't satisfied.

11. I love changing jobs! It's like starting with a _____.

Answers:

1. Time will tell

2. see it to believe it

3. no kidding

4. got canned

5. splashing out

6. blessing in disguise

7. live within her means

8. financial woes

9. lickety-split

10. in no time

11. clean slate

Set #17: Call it a Day

Dialogue

Jerry: I'm so tired. Let's **call it a day** and grab some dinner. It's **my treat**.

Linda: Sure, I'd love to but only if we **go dutch**. You pay way too often for me!

Jerry: Sure, if you insist. Let's check out that dessert place. They have sandwiches and then I can satisfy my **sweet tooth**. They have some decadent treats.

Linda: Sounds good. And don't just pick up the bill when I'm in the bathroom. I want to **pony up** for my share, okay?

Jerry: Let's **make a break for it** before Tony finds more work for us to do!

Linda: Sure, let's **head out.**

Vocabulary

Call it a day: To stop working.

Go dutch: To pay for yourself, especially at a restaurant or bar where everyone pays for their own foods or drinks. Or, on a date where both people pay for themselves.

Pony up: To get money/credit cards out to pay for something.

Sweet tooth: To like sugary foods.

My treat: To offer to pay, usually for a meal or drink.

Make a break for it: Leave somewhere quickly.

Head out: To go somewhere.

Exercise

Fill in the blanks with the correct phrase or idiom

1. I feel uncomfortable when guys always pay for me so I insist that we _____.

2. It's time to _____ for all those drinks you had!

3. I have a wicked _____ and can't stop eating candy.

4. Let's _____. I'm beat.

5. It's time to _____ and go home while the boss isn't looking.

6. Let's grab lunch. _____.

7. I'm tired. I'm going to _____ now.

Answers:

1. go dutch

2. pony up

3. sweet tooth

4. call it a day

5. make a break for it

6. My treat

7. head out

Set #18: Let Someone Off the Hook

Dialogue

Jerry: I'm worried about my job. A **storm is brewing** at my company. They were **let off the hook** last time but I'm not sure the other company won't sue for **breach of contract** this time.

Linda: I mean, **it takes two to tango.** That other company should have seen the **writing on the wall** way earlier than now. Your company missed so many deadlines.

Jerry: I know, it's **an impossible task.** I did my best but it's not going to be enough.

Linda: **Ditch that sinking ship.** Time to move onto bigger and better things.

Jerry: You're right. I'm **working my connections** already to **see what's out there**.

Vocabulary

Let off the hook: To not be punished, even though he/she was caught doing something wrong. For example, a politician who doesn't go to jail even though he committed a crime.

A storm is brewing: Knowing that there will be trouble in the future.

It takes two to tango: There are two people who are responsible for a situation or problem.

Breach of contract: Breaking the terms in a contract.

Writing on the wall: Something that is obvious, usually something negative.

An impossible task: Something that isn't able to be completed.

Ditch that sinking ship: To leave a bad situation.

Working my connections: Talking to people you know to get something from them.

See what's out there: To look for new opportunities.

Exercise

Fill in the blanks with the correct phrase or idiom

1. Maybe it's just me but I predict that _____ at work.

2. I quit before I could get fired because I saw the _____.

3. I couldn't believe that my son was _____ for that thing he did at school. Lucky guy.

4. Well, it's partly my fault but _____.

5. Honestly, that was _____ and not even Superman could have finished it.

6. It's time to _____ and find a better job.

7. That company is famous for not keeping their word, but I still didn't think a _____ would happen to me.

8. I'm going to start _____ to hopefully get an internship opportunity.

9. I'm not looking for a new job but I'm going to _____.

Answers:

1. a storm is brewing

2. writing on the wall

3. let off the hook

4. it takes two to tango

5. an impossible task

6. ditch that sinking ship

7. breach of contract

8. working my connections

9. see what's out there

Set #19: No Pain No Gain

Dialogue

Jerry: I'm thinking about going back to school! **Hitting the books** again. Am I crazy?

Linda: Well, as I like to say, "**No pain, no gain!**" If you're going to **make some bank** at a new job afterwards, then why not?

Jerry: That's what I thought too. I'm going to enjoy the **calm before the storm** though. I'm going to be **as busy as a beaver** once it starts up in September.

Linda: Oh, you'll **weather the storm** just fine. You've got a **good head on your shoulders**.

Vocabulary

No pain, no gain: Working hard for something.

Calm before the storm: A quiet period before a difficult period of time.

Weather the storm: Make it through, or survive a difficult situation.

Hitting the books: Studying.

Make some bank: To earn lots of money.

Good head on your shoulders: Smart/intelligent.

As busy as a beaver: Working a lot or very hard.

Exercise

Fill in the blanks with the correct phrase or idiom

1. I'm going to work up in northern Canada to _____.

2. Sorry, I can't hang out. I'll be _____ this weekend.

3. I'm just going to enjoy the _____ before things get too crazy at work.

4. I'm trying to get in shape by training for a marathon. It's tough going but _____.

5. You have a _____. You'll be fine at university.

6. It's going to take more than that to _____.

7. He's _____ with that new course he's taking.

Answers:

1. make some bank

2. hitting the books

3. calm before the storm

4. no pain, no gain

5. good head on your shoulders

6. weather the storm

7. as busy as a beaver

43

Set #20: Bite the Bullet

Dialogue

Jerry: Hey Linda, so I decided to finally **bite the bullet** and get a new car.

Linda: Oh wow! Did it **break the bank**?

Jerry: Kind of, but I didn't want another **lemon**.

Linda: I know, **when it rains, it pours,** right? Your car was always in the shop!

Jerry: For real. It was so annoying. Now, I just have to **crack the whip** on my employees to get out there and make more money for me to pay for it.

Linda: Don't **discredit** yourself! You're **working your fingers to the bone** too.

Vocabulary

Bite the bullet: Doing something that you've been avoiding for a while. For example, someone finally deciding to paint their house after delaying for years.

When it rains, it pours: When more than one bad thing happens at the same time.

Crack the whip: To be tough on someone.

Break the bank: Something that costs a lot.

A lemon: A reference to a car that needs more repairs than usual.

Discredit: Not give someone credit.

Working your fingers to the bone: Working very hard, beyond capacity.

Exercise

Fill in the blanks with the correct phrase or idiom

1. I wish he'd just _____ and stop complaining so much!

2. My mom used to _____ and make us all clean the house every Sunday morning.

3. That guy has the worst luck! _____.

4. I hope this new-to-me car I just bought isn't _____.

5. Let's go on a nice vacation but I don't want to _____.

6. I don't want to _____ his success, but his father handed him the job.

7. Take a break Tom! You're _____ lately.

Answers:

1. bite the bullet

2. crack the whip

3. When it rain, it pours

4. a lemon

5. break the bank

6. discredit

7. working your fingers to the bone

Set #21: Getting a Taste of His Own Medicine

Dialogue

Jerry: My son **got a taste of his own medicine** this weekend. He just barely escaped legal trouble **by the skin of his teeth**.

Linda: Seriously? What happened?

Jerry: Well, if you can believe it, someone called in a **noise complaint** to the **cops**. He's usually the one **tattling** on everyone else.

Linda: What was he doing?

Jerry: Just having a small **shindig** but I guess his neighbors were tired of the cops always showing up at their house for minor things.

Linda: Well, it seems like **sweet justice to me!**

Vocabulary

Got a taste of his own medicine: Being treated in the same bad way he/she has treated other people.

By the skin of his teeth: Just barely making it.

Noise complaint: Calling the police or authorities when neighbors are too loud.

Tattling: Telling on other people in an annoying way.

Cops: Another name for police.

Shindig: Party.

Sweet justice: When someone deserves what they get.

Exercise

Fill in the blanks with the correct phrase or idiom

1. I filed a _____ recently on my neighbor after they hosted a late-night party.

2. Let's have a little _____ to celebrate your birthday.

3. I had to call the _____ because I saw someone steal a car.

4. I'm so relieved that he _____ after bullying people for so many years.

5. Ahhh _____! That guy sure had it coming.

6. As a rule, I don't think _____ is a good thing but this guy deserved it.

7. He narrowly escaped that latest disaster _____.

Answers:

1. noise complaint

2. shindig

3. cops

4. got a taste of his own medicine

5. sweet justice

6. tattling

7. by the skin of his teeth

Set #22: Giving Someone the Cold Shoulder

Dialogue

Jerry: My daughter called me for the first time **in ages**. She usually **gives me the cold shoulder**.

Linda: Why? What happened to your relationship?

Jerry: Well, we got in a big fight about paying for **grad school.** She was **counting her chickens before they hatch** and assumed I would pay. But, I just didn't have **the dough**. That new car I bought **cost a pretty penny**.

Linda: Yeah, my son only calls **once in a blue moon**. He usually wants some **moola** too! But to be fair, he never misses a Mother's Day card.

Jerry: Kids these days! That seems like the **bare minimum**!

Vocabulary

Gives me the cold shoulder: To ignore someone.

Once in a blue moon: Rarely.

Counting her chickens before they hatch: Counting on something before it's already happened. For example, making plans to go to a certain university before getting the official acceptance letter.

In ages: In a long time.

Grad school: Graduate school.

The dough: Money.

Moola: Money.

Bare minimum: The least someone is obligated to do.

Cost a pretty penny: To be expensive.

Exercise

Fill in the blanks with the correct phrase or idiom

1. I wish my kids would do more than the _____ to keep the house clean and tidy.

2. I haven't seen my parents _____ because of Covid.

3. I play tennis _____ because it's always rainy where I live.

4. My neighbour has been _____ lately but I'm not sure why.

5. My daughter is convinced that she'll get into Harvard but I keep telling her to stop _____.

6. I wish that I'd gone to _____ right after I'd finished university.

7. My brother makes the big _____.

8. Give me _____ please!

9. My university education _____. I hope it was worth it!

Answers:

1. bare minimum

2. in ages

3. once in a blue moon

4. giving me the cold shoulder

5. counting her chicken before they hatch

6. grad school

7. moola

8. the dough

9. cost a pretty penny

Set #23: The Last Straw

Dialogue

Jerry: So I think I'm going to **leave my wife**.

Linda: On no! What happened? You guys always seemed like pretty **happy campers** to me.

Jerry: Well, **the last straw** was looking at my retirement accounts and seeing that most of them were **cleaned out**. Plus, we're in the red on all our other accounts too. She loves to **shop till she drops** but I didn't realize how **dire** it was until now.

Linda: Sorry to hear that. I hope you can get back **in the black**. You went **from rags to riches** once. I'm sure you can do it again.

Jerry: Hopefully, but after paying the divorce lawyers, I'll have a lot of work to **make up for lost time** on those retirement accounts. And she may also want **spousal support.**

Linda: Well, hang in there my friend. I'm here for you.

Vocabulary

The last straw: The final annoying thing before someone loses their patience. For example, a child has been misbehaving all day but his dad finally yelled at him when he wouldn't stay in his room at bedtime.

In the black: To not be in debt.

Leave my wife: Separate or get a divorce.

Happy campers: People that are joyful or having fun together.

Cleaned out: Usually refers to money, when someone spends everything.

Shop till she drops: Loves shopping and spends lots of time doing it.

Dire: Very bad.

Make up for lost time: Wasted time that you can't get back.

Spousal support: Money paid to a former husband or wife after getting divorced.

From rags to riches: Poor to rich.

Exercise

Fill in the blanks with the correct phrase or idiom

1. The food situation is now becoming _____. One of us has to go shopping!

2. Honestly, this is _____ before he gets fired.

3. We started living frugally and are now _____.

4. I want to _____. We just don't have that much in common anymore.

5. The kids were such _____ when I bought them a new trampoline.

6. My wife loves to _____ but I feel nervous about how much money she's spending.

7. I had to pay _____ after getting divorced.

8. I only started dating in my twenties. Now, I have to _____.

9. Wow! I love the story of that guy going _____ when he moved to the USA.

Answers:

1. dire

2. the last straw

3. in the black

4. leave my wife

5. happy campers

6. shop till she drops

7. spousal support

8. make up for lost time

9. from rags to riches

Set #24: The Elephant in the Room

Dialogue

Jerry: I'm ready to **blow a gasket** at work. Nobody wants to talk about **the elephant in the room**.

Linda: Oh yeah? What's going on?

Jerry: Well, the project manager at my company is not **on the ball.** We keep talking about budgets and timelines but the reality is that this guy should **get canned.** Everything goes through him but it's like **pulling teeth** to get anything done because of it.

Linda: It sounds like you guys are **getting into deep water**. Will your client **bail**?

Jerry: I'm starting to wonder. If I was **in their shoes**, I'd certainly demand a change. They're **bleeding money** right now because of it.

Linda: Tough times. I'm curious to see what happens.

Vocabulary

The elephant in the room: Something obvious and important that nobody wants to talk about.

On the ball: Easily understands things or reacts quickly to a situation.

Getting into deep water: To be in trouble.

Get canned: Fired from a job.

Blow a gasket: Get very angry or annoyed.

Pulling teeth: Something painful or difficult to do.

Bail: To leave or exit quickly, to give up on something.

In their shoes: To consider someone else's position or way or thinking.

Bleeding money: Losing money very quickly.

Exercise

Fill in the blanks with the correct phrase or idiom

1. Honestly, my job would be decent if the company wasn't _____.

2. It's time to _____! I'm nervous that someone is going to call the police.

3. My brother might _____ because he's always leaving early.

4. Everyone is beating around the bush talking about unimportant stuff. But, I wish I had enough courage to mention _____.

5. He's _____ with all his financial commitments.

6. My boss is _____, unlike the last guy.

7. My dad is usually a pretty relaxed guy but sometimes he'd _____ over something minor.

8. It's honestly like _____ to get any information out of him.

9. Before judging, try to put yourself _____.

Answers:

1. bleeding money

2. bail

3. get canned

4. the elephant in the room

5. getting into deep water

6. on the ball

7. blow a gasket

8. pulling teeth

9. in their shoes

Set #25: Stealing Someone's Thunder

Dialogue

Jerry: I just had a big fight with my friend and I'm not sure I can just **get over it.** It was a **massive blow-up.**

Linda: Oh no! What happened?

Jerry: Well, she's my co-worker and keeps **stealing my thunder** on work projects. She's taking credit for stuff that I do. I'm **sick and tired of it.**

Linda: That's a **tough pill to swallow**. I'd for sure have a **bee in my bonnet** about this too.

Jerry: It's not even **the straw that broke the camel's back.** She owes me a thousand **bucks** as well.

Linda: It sounds like you two need a bit of distance from each other.

Vocabulary

Stealing my thunder: Taking credit for something that someone else did.

Get over it: To fully recover (from an illness) or not think about it negatively anymore (break-up with a girlfriend or boyfriend, losing a job, etc.).

Tough pill to swallow: Something difficult to get over.

Bee in my bonnet: A certain issue that is annoying someone.

The straw that broke the camel's back: The last thing in a series of bad things before an event occurs — like a breakup, quitting a job, or fight.

Blow-up: Big fight or problem.

Massive: Very big/huge.

Sick and tired of it: Annoyed by something that happens frequently.

Bucks: Dollars.

Exercise

Fill in the blanks with the correct phrase or idiom

1. He looks like a million _____ these days.

2. I get a _____ any time I deal with that certain customer at work.

3. My mom is pretty relaxed but she would have a big _____ every once in a while.

4. He got a _____ raise at work. Lucky guy!

5. My teammate keeps _____ and always seems to forget that I set him up for most of his goals.

6. Getting a D on that test was a _____.

7. I can't just _____. I'm still in love with my ex-boyfriend.

8. That last project was _____ before I quit.

9. My mom is _____. She's gone on strike!

Answers:

1. bucks

2. bee in my bonnet

3. blow-up

4. massive

5. stealing my thunder

6. tough pill to swallow

7. get over it

8. the straw that broke the camel's back

9. sick and tired of it

Set #26: Hit the Books

Dialogue

Jerry: I've been **breaking out in a cold sweat** a lot lately. I'm not used to having to **hit the books**.

Linda: What are you studying for?

Jerry: I have to pass this exam for work and I'll lose my job if I don't. I'm maybe **making a mountain of a molehill** but I can't help being nervous about it. It's been so long since I've had to take a test.

Linda: It's **like riding a bike**. You'll get back into it once you start. **Go with the flow**.

Jerry: Do you have any **study tips**?

Linda: My best advice is to study a little bit every day instead of **pulling all-nighters** or **cramming**. That doesn't work.

Vocabulary

Breaking out in a cold sweat: To be afraid or nervous about something.

Hit the books: When someone spends time studying.

Go with the flow: To relax and go along with whatever.

Making a mountain out of a molehill: To make something into a bigger deal than it is. For example, someone who loses sleep over a small problem.

Like riding a bike: Something that you always remember how to do, even with a large break in between.

Study tips: Ideas for how to study more effectively.

Pulling all-nighters: Staying up all night to study or work.

Cramming: Trying to learn everything for a test at the last minute.

Exercise

Fill in the blanks with the correct phrase or idiom

1. Dude, sorry I can't hang out. I need to _____.

2. You'll get the hang of it. It's _____.

3. Before the second date, I kept _____. That's a bad sign, right?

4. I think you need to _____ with this school project. It sounds like you're taking it way more seriously than the other people in your group.

5. I don't think that _____ is a very effective study method.

6. One of the best _____ is to do it for one hour and then take a 10-minute break.

7. My days of _____ are over. I'm too old for that!

8. I think you're _____. It's not a big deal!

Answers:

1. hit the books

2. like riding a bike

3. breaking out in a cold sweat

4. go with the flow

5. cramming

6. study tips

7. pulling all-nighters

8. making a mountain out of a molehill

Set #27: Hit the Sack

Dialogue

Jerry: I have to **hit the sack.** I'm so tired right now.

Linda: Have you been **burning the midnight oil** lately?

Jerry: Yeah, I've been trying to study for this test. I got a slow start working on it because I was in the hospital for a few days.

Linda: Well, **better late than never**. But, you need to go to bed early and get enough sleep. If you're tired, you won't retain anything that you've studied.

Jerry: You're right. It was **many moons** ago that I got a decent night's sleep.

Linda: **Keep fighting**! I think you'll **ace** it.

Jerry: Well, here's hoping I **come up trumps**! Time to **knuckle down** and get to work.

Vocabulary

Hit the sack: Go to bed.

Many moons: A long time ago.

Burning the midnight oil: Staying up late working or studying.

Better late than never: Encouragement after getting a late start to something.

Keep fighting: Keep trying.

Ace: To get a high mark on a test or do well at something like a job interview.

Come up trumps: To get exactly what is needed at the last minute.

Knuckle down: To focus deeply on something.

Exercise

Fill in the blanks with the correct phrase or idiom

1. Don't forget to _____ early. It's your big game tomorrow!

2. I know it's difficult but ____. Things will get better.

3. Although it was _____ ago, I still think about my ex-boyfriend.

4. I've been _____ lately, working a second job.

5. Honestly, it's _____ but he dropped the ball on this project.

6. You won't _____ the test unless you study.

7. That guy has an uncanny ability to always _____.

8. It's the last thing I want to do but I know it's time to _____ and study.

Answers:

1. hit the sack

2. keep fighting

3. many moons

4. burning the midnight oil

5. better late than never

6. ace

7. come up trumps

8. knuckle down

Set #28: Twist My Arm

Dialogue

Jerry: Okay, fine Linda, **twist my arm**. I'll go get a drink with you.

Linda: Wait, what? You want to grab a drink? Sure, why not. I'd love to **unwind.**

Jerry: Yeah, I'm having a rough time at work. I just found out that one of my coworkers **got a kickback** on this latest contract. Some bad stuff is **going down.**

Linda: Oh wow. That's not good. Let's **kick back and relax**. I know a new place that has some great **craft beer**.

Jerry: Yeah, it's just the **tip of the iceberg**. A whole bunch of money **vanished into thin air** too.

Linda: Oh, wow Jerry! You need to **take a breather.** Meet you at Brown's Pub in 20!

Vocabulary

Twist my arm: Someone has convinced you to make a different decision.

Got a kickback: Accepted a bribe.

Tip of the iceberg: A very small part of something much bigger, usually a negative thing or a problem.

Vanished into thin air: Disappeared without a trace.

Going down: Happening.

Unwind: Relax.

Kick back and relax: Chill out.

Craft beer: Specialty beer that is brewed in small batches.

Take a breather: Relax for a while.

Exercise

Fill in the blanks with the correct phrase or idiom

1. There's some crazy stuff _____ in the US election.

2. I can't believe your friend just _____.

3. The politician _____ for awarding the contract to a certain company.

4. Well, that's just the _____. There's a whole lot more that we don't know yet.

5. My coworkers always have to _____ to get me to go for a drink with them but I'm always happy that I did.

6. I used to drink _____ but it's too expensive now that I've lost my job!

7. I like to watch some Netflix to _____ from the week.

8. My dad loves to _____ with a nice beer on Friday nights.

9. Let's go outside and _____.

Answers:

1. going down

2. vanished into thin air

3. got a kickback

4. tip of the iceberg

5. twist my arm

6. craft beer

7. unwind

8. kick back and relax

9. take a breather

Set #29: Stab Someone in the Back

Dialogue

Jerry: Oh wow. I had a rough week at work.

Linda: What happened?

Jerry: Well, I usually like to **bury my head in the sand** and not pay attention to **office gossip** but Tim **stabbed someone in the back**.

Linda: Who?

Jerry: It was his boss.

Linda: Oh wow! Well, **let the dust settle**. I'm sure they won't be like **two peas in a pod** but hopefully, they can **put it behind** them.

Jerry: Tim isn't known for **letting bygones be bygones** but we'll see how it goes. I'm honestly just **counting the days** until this **blows over**.

Vocabulary

Stabbed someone in the back: To betray someone, especially someone with a close relationship.

Bury my head in the sand: To avoid a certain situation or problem.

Let the dust settle: Waiting for a situation to become calm or normal after something exciting or unusual happened.

Two peas in a pod: Two people who are very similar in thinking or appearance.

Put it behind: Overcome, or forget about it.

Office gossip: Talking behind someone's back at work, rumours.

Letting bygones be bygones: Putting something behind you, forgiving.

Counting the days: Waiting for something to be finished.

Blows over: A bad time passes or is finished.

Exercise

Fill in the blanks with the correct phrase or idiom

1. My sister and I were like _____ growing up.

2. I actively try to avoid _____.

3. I think you two can get back together. Just _____ for a bit.

4. One of the only things I regret in life is the time that I _____.

5. I know it sounds crazy, but I can't let it go and _____ me.

6. I don't want to but I tend to _____ and not get involved with conflict.

7. It's really impressive how good my mom is at _____.

8. I hope this _____ quickly. I'm so tired of the drama.

9. I'm _____ until I can retire. I hate my job.

Answers:

1. two peas in a pod

2. office gossip

3. let the dust settle

4. stabbed someone in the back

5. put it behind

6. bury my head in the sand

7. letting bygones be bygones

8. blows over

9. counting the days

Set #30: Sit Tight

Dialogue

Jerry: Hey, let's get moving! **Time is money.**

Linda: **Sit tight.** I need to grab a few things before we go.

Jerry: Come on. I'm caught **between a rock and a hard place**. We have to get to the train station on time. I hate always being the **bad guy** about stuff like this.

Linda: Well, to be fair, you've been as **clear as mud** about exactly what time we need to leave though. The time you tell me keeps changing and I don't think traffic will be as bad as you think.

Jerry: There are always a ton of **traffic jams** between here and there. Let's **get a move on.**

Linda: Okay, **get off my back**! I'll be ready **in the blink of an eye.**

Vocabulary

Sit tight: Wait patiently and don't take any action right now.

Clear as mud: Confusing or not easy to understand.

Between a rock and a hard place: having two bad options to choose from.

Time is money: To try to get someone to work faster or more efficiently.

Traffic jams: When cars aren't moving quickly because it's busy.

Get a move on: Hurry up.

Bad guy: Someone who always has bad news/enforces a rule.

Get off my back: Leave me alone; stop bugging me.

In the blink of an eye: In a short amount of time.

Exercise

Fill in the blanks with the correct phrase or idiom

1. If you leave after 8am, there will be lots of _____.

2. Let's _____. I don't want to be late for school.

3. I try to always remember that _____.

4. I had a terrible teacher in high school. His explanations were as _____.

5. _____ while I check and see what time the movie starts.

6. My dad is really stuck _____ with this new project he agreed to take on.

7. I hate to be the _____ but you really need to get it together or you're going to get fired.

8. Don't miss the eclipse. It'll happen _____.

9. I wish my boss would _____.

Answers:

1. traffic jams

2. get a move on

3. time is money

4. clear as mud

5. Sit tight

6. between a rock and a hard place

7. bad guy

8. in the blink of an eye

9. get off my back

Before You Go

If you found this book useful, please leave a review wherever you bought it. It will help other English learners, like yourself find this resource.

CPSIA information can be obtained
at www.ICGtesting.com
Printed in the USA
LVHW051149070721
691974LV00007B/256